THICKETS
SWAMPED
IN
FENCE-COATED
BRIARS

EVAN GRAY

Garden-Door Press
Ithaca, NY

Copyright © 2023 Evan Gray
All rights reserved
Printed in the United States of America
First edition, 2023

ISBN # 979-8-9886822-0-2
Text set in Adobe Jenson Pro, titles in Orpheus.

Printed with Arcadian ink.

www.garden-doorpress.com

for my family

*"Our walk at noon, with branches overgrown,
That mock our scant manuring, and require
More hands than ours to lop their wanton growth:
Those blossoms also, and those dropping gums,
That lie bestrown unsightly and unsmooth,
Ask riddance, if we mean to treat with ease;
Meanwhile, as nature wills, night bids us rest."'*

– John Milton, *Paradise Lost*

If you live near the hills, near where people use their hands, near where the days are hounding and long, where the screams inside your chest belt and buckle your knees, where your hands ache when you lay down, and when you close your eyes, you can hear sirens over the ridgeline.

Pale green colors flicker, tracing a field bush-hogged & wounded. We become cut with language and weight damaging rain. Words, lay sad behind my tongue. Words, form the abandoned racetrack: a distorted and disfigured mile-marker of me. Might you be home to one more good time, video reunions of fathers coming home from Afghanistan play on perpetual loop.

I see the gleam of lines of the highway late in the afternoon after rain. I see my dementia-plagued grandmother. I pretend I am the shadowed figures cast on the rock foundation of my childhood basement. O, and the crows—lining the fence to the trailer park.

Rest is punctuated by the impending. We go back to work or sit down for a second or catch our breaths or go find something else to fix. At the house, we tell this funny little joke about life: everyone who dies also goes to work.

BE HIND SIGHT

I

hills spring in setting sun
flying kites in cow pastures   the mine
a fossil of *activity moves through*
tire swinging wind

II

cycled down emotion as result
~~what seems is only is~~ [must've been told too many times]
Cherokee spirit gift shop
pond ripples
~~they're~~ [there] all my life

III

hemlock one limb bent finger
~~tries to move but can't~~ [no wind]
coon caught in a bear trap
farm window under porch white lattice
eyes each a marble of wind trumped thunder

IV

tax collectors called first thing
gas station scratch-off
shimmering some old man's bracelet
headlight pushing through fog

V

Christmas came on [Tuesday]
after the money's spent
weight of blood trail in laurels
only a fraction of cold
spinning up the flurries

VI

light oak embers
gas station scratch-offs
couple squirrels at the feeder
how many more are left

This book, being about work is, by its very nature, about violence—to the spirit as well as to the body.

Look at his hands. Look at the underpaid. Look at the farmland. Look at the greedy cops that ride our asses. Nothing is good that doesn't bleed. It is grueling and unrewarding, work and life. I think of this as I am sanding an ambulance box, listening to a podcast. A music video. A valley of unturned copse. One singular machine embodies more endless machines. In the country and in the city, machines are now all we have. The whining of the sander. The purity of the air hose. The groan of a radio and how much of my life is waiting on the machine to take over. I type into my phone until the machine malfunctions, until the pipes are clogged, until we jam it up, then we cuss it, too.

Can we ache for the combines, the engines, the mowers, the tillers, the sanders, the air hoses, the endless, the rest? Are we allowed to be welded together, to work for them, as the rust or dirt or corrosion is sanded off and thrown into the daylight? You can't win for losing sometimes, my dad would often say. He would say this when he was frustrated in work or life. He would say this after my mom scratched a lottery ticket. He would say this after giving the blessing for we are grateful beyond the holy machines.

windowed patterns of clouds
breathing trotlines
cat fishermen trolling tangled
in the pier, gleaming twitter
cinderblocks tied to a post
face in the card flapping wind
unnamed boy drowned here
over a week ago

My parents bought our now-family-home in the middle of the Great Recession. Prior to this house, we moved each year—house to house, cabin to house. All around the same mountain town. The mold of the one I remember the most used to make me itch, used to make my throat swell. Still, the basement was holy. I would rub my human toes through the mildewed fringe carpet from the 70s. Each home was ours. But when we got to this house, my mom was excited to grow a garden.

Her and dad staked out a plot—20 feet long, 10 feet wide—where they could plant lettuce, tomatoes, and squash up front, green beans, potatoes, and corn in the back. The garden grew well for two years. I helped out when I was home.

It was spring when it happened. It was fall when I remembered. We stood outside of a funeral home in the rain and told stories about how lucky we were to be relatively healthy. Your hair was blonde in the wind. We were alive then. You were in my dream wading through the tunnel culvert holding the head of a rabbit in your paw. You had no mouth or teeth. Your hair was tied to the bridge. Your name was carved in the oak. It was all I had left to remember you by.

Outside on my lunch break: I stare into the distance and ache.

oaks, hickories, maples, pine   woods pond im-
parted   brightness
                                        breaking through
        hillsides

                                                sound of

thawing
                                        we are daily
a day out of willow catkins

paths   before us,   wood, weather-stain
glaring   color of color

the color   color of

        sky-color air

Thomasville Furniture Factory boomed during my grade school years, and I can remember sitting on the brick retaining wall—during sunny days when our teachers rewarded us with sunlight—and staring across the parking lot of the school where the factory set, watching the smoke clear over the mill and hang like a shadow over Bluff Mountain in the distance. Denny's mother worked at the factory and every so often, during PE, he would try to escape and run toward her, imagining she would be waiting for his embrace: happy, whole, and angelic. Denny would always get caught before he could make it off the playground or out of the tennis courts. He would yell in his high-pitched, seven-year-old voice, "I can leave if I want to."

All the folks that had come to work there for years stopped coming. I didn't understand at the time but just noticed things seemed to be quieter at the factory: fewer cars, less smoke, no PA announcements. We could hear their pages over the loudspeaker when our classroom windows were cracked.

It was spring.

Then the bridge washed out and the river never stopped moving.

Your high school baseball jersey hanging at the BBQ restaurant.

Antlered deer beside definitions of words like *family* and *Sunday*.

In the woods the hills just wither tectonically.

THE YEAR THE COLORS OF THE HIGH-TOP
MOUNTAINS WERE TORCHED

I.

in a barn loft
at your house I didn't know how
the first time I saw a woman's breasts
the first time I had a panic attack
the holy spirit left my body
then perched in a deer stand
I waded the thicket
I became a mange ridden yearling buck stuck with several arrows
I breathed like an animal
I exhaled through my fish gill cheeks
bones of the dead tangled in the telephone wire of a gully
from the road the barn wore a shape of your face
barn like a vacuum of all youth
sunken into the acute angles
of each rafter

II.

I was I was I was I was I was
I was I was I was I was I was
was I was I was I was I was
I was I was I was I was I was
I was I was I was I was I was
was I was I was I was I was
I was I was I was I was I was
I was I was I was I was I was
was I was I was I was I was
I was I was I was I was I was
I was I was I was I was I was
was I was I was I was I was
I was I was I was I was I was
I was I was I was I was I was
was I was I was I was I was
I was I was I was I was I was
I was I was I was I was I was
was I was I was I was I was
I was I was I was I was I was
I was I was I was I was I was
was I was I was I was I was
I was I was I was I was I was
I was I was I was I was I was
was I was I was I was I was

III.

I was what I was forbidden from

I was the river bank before it was eroded

I was I was I was

I was told there is no single path no mountain cutback no garden

I was I was I was

I was held unto the light as all humans

lukewarm and gutted I stumbled through the thicket

men with flashlights led me to a makeshift altar in the pines

told me I was I was I was I was being released

shadows moved under everyone's floorboard eyes

IV.

minnows school up

under a few laurels

spring feeds into this creek

where the bridge was

before I was born

V.

after I began to drink I also began to deer hunt
deer hunting became ministry and a keepsake

to talk at school about how big the last one was
I have never shot an identifiable male with gnarled horns

I have worn horns on my head that cover my face
I have filled Mountain Dew bottles with dip spit

I have walked these mountains before the football games
I have climbed the tallest one in this county and spit from its peak

no trespassing signs have sung to me
they have been melodies of a lost dream

VI.

even now I am awakened from dreams of trophy horns
mounted above the bed I sleep in
in these dreams I am not afraid of pleasure

I am a confident solider of feral creatures
I am a mover of all bodies   animal or other

hold your breath and see how far you can run

below the
surface

          low pond
   light

         drowned
old wheels

what direction to ourselves
        might we find, hay picks
        old parts of barn shutters nailed to the wall
                firewood to unload

a hill reflected in snowmelt puddles
        leaks in the door

from here mountains part back
        the sun hum of diesel trucks
                matte black against the fender

dogs barking at their own
        shadows of a father outside
                the courthouse birds pecking
        for seed over snow

not to outshine frozen layers
        roughed up laurels from deer horns
                jake brakes vibrate through my bones
hills of vine semi cut green
        fauna dangle too numb to notice

        my ears
        my feet
        a patch quilt

Alternative Headline 1: Bare Branches were Torched in the Evening Wind by Venture Capitalists

Alternative Headline 2: Foliage as Empty as a Fawn: Makes a Great Hotel!

Alternative Headline 3: A Stranger Bore Your Eyes, The Black Lunged Miners, How They Pray to Not Hurt Any Longer

Alternative Headline 4: Ways to Survive Extraction, Take Too Much Sinus Medication and Watch Documentaries

That is the type of abandonment we hear and see and read. And the people are victims of this physiological hijacking. Maybe this is what causes the guilt. Maybe, therefore, the farms are bought out. Maybe this destruction happens internally but projected in the landscape. Cut, scissor, jig-sawed, but restlessly expected to give, both land and people give.

TOYOTA

the center
murky mirror of

clouds.

he shot
himself against
the front tire;

a new private
property sign.

At the BBQ restaurant, we imagine we are in a romantic and rural place, with antlered deer
mounted on the wall. In the woods, the tectonic plates eek. To ignore a chain bank beside us,
the aching in our head, tomorrow is Monday or even worse.

Hank hums a melody on the radio

Everywhere I see is something mistaken for photography

Springleaf Financial ads strung up in the pines

Memory forgotten how to get back to

To the right of the garden was

an arching white oak, which is now

as I'm looking at it

swaying as a thunderstorm

comes closing in.

OF LEAVES

        I MARK   DECLINE

          the sounds

               dying

You'll find yourself just listening, the story you have heard over a dozen times.

You just listen.

You listen for moments that mark continuity, deviation, and connection.

Your stories become intermingled with others.

Some you've heard. Some you've invented.

glass projecting my face   when I stare hours alone light

behind yesterday's   eyes going back & forth

to be wild   to conquer some sort of   direction further

birds crash into the window   flashes of sight   before noise

orange coated wings spot on
                              my eye   *disorder is another*

order end of   the day singing whispers earth

worms crawling sucked in a vacuum   old spruce left there

and then I laid myself to rest with
words of below this ground lies
a man with only one true home
that he could remember, a screen
door of which he has ran into
nearly a dozen times, chasing
nothing of which he can recall
still he remembers the ones who
have said poor people abuse the
system like his uncle his night at
the gambling barge set up by the
used car lot, it takes its toll on
his body his hepatitis his spots
on his liver as dark and pooled as
swamped rainwater in the gully of
highway 88 in April just past the
junkyard where cars are buried
in the creek and you can see
their headlights the 75 Pontiac
the Ford Geo looking out at you
tracing you on the way home from
baseball practice just past Devil's
Stairs a rock formation that was
laid up by the state on accident
when they started to pave that
mountain and ran out of money

buds   late dead

selves   window,
                        heard
                        ground,

        masses of
        wild bees.

and now is the point in which
I worry about immense debt
and worry about having a job
and worry about moving across
the country and worry that I
have a brain tumor or just worry
about worrying you worry too
much about this and what is the
destruction of man (man) or the
destruction of the land too for
even when I close my eyes I can
see the rain closing in summer of
never ending rain over three-top
peak where the torturous roads
scare my aunt to detour and where
the creek lets me know I am man
for my legs aren't as steady and
my grip of toes attempt to claw
through my wading boots and
later holding an axe which seems
to be an attempt to measure the
world like the way my father holds
a piece of wood before he cuts
and this section is now broken
and I am worrying again about
destruction and breaking down
my hands are hurting and knees
are swelling wider than ditches

CHANGE, EROSION

in rows   of some corn
field. shading   accidents:

my bones to   become
unnamed animal   bones

by the old
swing set.

Why do we try to live sometimes inside a broken machine that is both animal and human, that is both man-made and organic, and why do my eyes burn so much when I walk outside in spring, and why is my father deathly allergic to horses and hay, and why did I just find out that my great uncle died in a coal mine in Clay County, West Virginia and why was my grandfather a coal miner, if only for a brief period of time, and is that why his lungs failed him.

There must be a fine weaver of lines who holds all my cards.

What is there to do other than to write more of this, more like this, steeped vein of myself and to others, for the destruction of man may be the self-destruction of all. The improvised understanding of what can make us think: ticking, ticking, running or not. The sky will fold and when Gabriel's trumpet blows and I worry will I may be the last to go, last to cut my human body open and be evaporated into the rays of blue sky.

All I can say is that would be nice. All I can say is I would settle to just be a laurel bush, a branch that waves back and forth only once in a while.

& all day rain outlines
every tree / new object

            month of grass evergreen

            trembling already me

            a new me gone

language now ice

itself reflected dusty wood
running roadside almost

At times, the I seems to be a sharp lens of connectivity, reminding the reader of tender and wrenching moments that we experience as a body, as a collective.

Fucked out of our money and the land spit it back at us. We are forgiven for what we do and
who is foraging. Whoever is in Ore Knob Mine has little to nothing to do with me. All life
begins as a cumshot slung from a native plant and nested into the eyes of the boss man. Man's
pores gurgle up unsigned checks and the pension of rest will be littered across this landscape.
Arcadia, no more. A peaceful existence for me of my kins, no more. Perhaps it lies along the
shores of the river we can't afford where cash billows up near some time-flooded headstones. So
long to the rest of everyone's paid vacation days. I will use the steel wool scrubber on my teeth
to nip away any evidence that I am responsible for.

There are so many revolutions light years away.

hallelujah to come   translated in rain

showers high grove tree-line figures

moon again lonesome bleak

shaped like a tractor bucket

horizon lines may outshine the flood light

art thou or aren't thou   lichen brick facing

hedge grass   fingernails blooded tooth aching

that old hymn you remember

Faces become personified invitations of investment opportunity, a grand-stand hotel. The current now puddles in clouds with rocking chairs implanted on the porch. Enough, just country enough to blow mine deep. Stirred & shaken with a conscious throbbing in the circumference of generations, an antique mall selling your grandmother's necklace as if it was pulsing out of a six-pack ring. Rock ruins begging for blood, my own inextricable blood of the backyard no longer. Where the shit tank leaked under the ground when it was full & me and the neighbor boys couldn't play ball there. Instead, we opted for the engine-dead bus sitting across the trailer park.

This is where I convinced the neighbor kids of magic. I ripped the salamander tail off and it grew back. I found arrowheads beside Budweiser cans. I dug ginseng roots and pretended I was a family member I had never met, and the trampoline I got for Christmas rested violently in a thicket of geraniums: earth's stale hands. I learned to hold myself up with the worn earth rust flaking off into the hollers. We were all pale empty symbols then: tv cords behind a dresser. And peace of mind was hung up on a gun rack or swimming in the river after the rain. If you could exchange this memory, you would. Dead strangers would not recognize you in their final hours of existence and corporations would all be burned.

I was   [nothing]

            morning but an axle handle

birds   leaned up against
light   canto
                    infinite

waked
dawning & heard of

Each summer, no matter how endless it seems, becomes invaded by frost. There's a section of the New River I fish out in Todd, NC. I can hear the fuzz of trucks and vans hauling canoes for tourists who've come to float through the shallow current. In my mind, it's summer. The water temperature is just slightly cooler here than in the main river. There's a healthy stocking of rainbow trout. A limb is waving as the truck goes by. I'm making sure my flies are floating. Nine people slow down and wave toward me. I've never seen them before in my life. I can feel how temporary this has become.

Today I stand in the rain during my break at work. I look up to the nameless mountain beside my father's shop and think about how green everything looks peeking through the midst. And what is one to do but bear it.

hiding in the wrong tree. the wrong
rope swing. hopeful guessing
strangling on the beauties of it &
nowhere can I place myself, no
other axis or ancestors. language
dirty scripts painted, carved in
glass, toward the river & other
mystifying areas: have you seen the
evening news about the bombings
and the fire that took R's cousin's
house. then comes the fog. Bird
nest in oak barrels & I am guilty
with the same temperate silence.
nights below the moon convoluted
self-messages recycled, emotions
that never spirit. self, me, a
hemisphere of rain saying nothing,
unconnected vapor. I lost my voice,
passing I think, any minute is never
anything like the words before it

The garden at my family home stopped growing two summers ago. The oak that towered beside the plot was infected with some sort of disease that poisoned the soil. Mom and I went to the town to get some treatment-based fertilizer that was supposed to neutralize it, to keep it from spreading. We tossed it on the ground, and it scorched our grass.

I dream my skin is peeling off my human-bone frame.

I dream I am stumbling through hell.

The moon is an arrowhead you get to hold in your hand.

ownership confused with action

places visited are not in acquisition I need

a little, little bit of help I wrote this

in the kitchen, I wrote this in the living room

I have ascended, I am writing this from on high

I am writing this now, I have left out something, let me

fix it, I need to remember, what will help

in each movement, a shed is mauled by snowstorms

in the way of the world

in the meaning, or used

in the myth, how do you

feel an atom bomb & try to not live forever

changed   object
seen: foregrounds of
                      others

red or
I

                      autumnal
                      hue

the day   setting
the eye   body

BARBED WIRE WILLOW FENCE

city folks turning to wind chimes
conversation translated AM frequencies of
sacred radio static   just behind the timber-

line   just behind the shadows

shed standing town reflected jade green

a steady mile marker, moss
north side of   a tree   a foot
from planted daffodils

I get afraid to go to sleep before 10:30 sometimes. I'm afraid I'll miss it, something that I've been waiting all day to happen. It could happen shortly after I turn in. For if I don't experience it, what good is it? Energy wasted. That is an unnatural thought. I remind myself of this as I write a few poems using various how-to garden manuals. Their language is about flowers, growth, moving, rain, and natural fertilizer. I use my words, and it feels like I had a say-so in what was going down. I realized I just held on and wound up here.

to be
present
to have
a perception
to perceive
to see
to feel
to know
to check
to cuckold
the self or other
your cell phone
on a walk
the magnolia is
the pasture is
waves
bending back
over
over the ridge
my mind
off there
somewhere
near
the lonely
the young
the lonely young lady
who drove off
it was foggy
it was suicide
it was not her fault
she couldn't drive
maybe
she was old

she was sad
maybe her brain
miscalculated
something
maybe it
wasn't there

AIRLESSNESS

we are born again
and tossed, born
again and tossed
born again
and drowned.

embryos
contrasted clouded
color of ice
my reflection

                                    me

a pane
          a sentence

wearing traces, caught in veins
waiting on,   time spots

                    some
                    one's mind

For whatever way you have taken to find yourself not guilty of feeling this just know this is the portrait.

Rotate the ridge into landscape position to peer into the oblong sun.

You are a banded-arrowhead on the surface.

You are still a dime a dozen.

You ache like this and no river can help fix it, no natural thing. I'm afraid we have fucked it away.

part of   of one
          another

impart

        so   so
            so   reap   row pines

                  o   o
        o   o

      o   o

screen door clapping

frames of a table

pain pills

on either side

missed child

support payments

mounted largemouth

bass held by

my thumb

will he call

will he show

up in court

who is going

to feed me or

take me in

if I eat this

will I get diabetes

if I use this

does it cause Alzheimer's

what are the chances

we die in this car crash

where do people

in the world take

comfort & this

hole in the tree

portal to God

of the darkest

parts of night

first black hole

photographed

in space

what do you see

when work has you

wrapped in a ball

rolling over the hill

do you think how

much you might miss

As I was driving home from work this week, I heard a line that supposedly Townes Van Zandt said when he was asked about his songwriting. "I want to write songs so good even I don't know what they're about."

Daniel Antopolsky, a musician that hung out on the fringes of Texas songwriters, did an interview with Townes. There's a famous photo of them all and Suzanna sitting on Guy's front porch playing music but since then, no one has really heard much of Daniel Antopolsky. In the interview, he recounts a terrifying moment with Townes. Daniel is quick to note that while he would smoke and snort and eat anything, he wouldn't shoot anything. Townes was much different, much more lonesome than perhaps anyone in that scene. Townes strapped a rubber band around his arm and said he needed to take a little nap. Daniel was with him when his nap went wrong and Townes's lips turned blue and shaking. He was afraid the cops would haul them both to jail for the drugs, so before he called for an ambulance, he tossed them into the bushes below the hotel. Townes barely lived and Daniel left the country for a while.

I'm too tired to write a poem about this.

My life is roughly a thousand mornings and my teeth are aching.

This is a state of mind, I say.

An offering of decay to rivers where the rock bass feed on the underside of leaves. We are stoned injecting dirt into our arteries and eyes. We are reminded of another narrative, new free blooming vigor, free from the can-crushing, the gnashing, and in this thought, you notice a potter flower cluster growing together.

They wrote their vows in the living room while the bank foreclosed on their home. Thistles from the state's fence posts were driven into the man's hands. Frozen over springs filled the ditches.

This, the temporariness of myth mixed with lymph nodes, the swelling stress of money, and tunnels in the mountains we pissed in without regard. Each thought produces a pattern more vigorous than the rain.

This is home, we notice, bundled tight in the truck bed. There are growing annuals and chainsaw repair shops. Windows as open as a mud stain.

The payoff is spiritual but you can't spend it.

But it's easy to make money when you've got it.

The construction company in my town grew from a one-man business.

It's easy to open your skull when you're dead.

In the evening, I wash my face and pick at the places the lacquer thinner dries out on my hands. I know that if I don't rest soon, tomorrow will be hard. There's a rhythmic process to the whole thing, my life, at this point. Gears are going.

And the rhythms last longer for people in the country. The rhythms are swaying around, buckling the knees but feeding the bellies. The hills are badly bruised.

I found you bound in the creek with rhododendron leaves stuffed in your mouth.

I want my soul there beside you.

Remember me, I yell, tied up in the kitchen-week-old garbage.

Me, asleep all night on the porch.

I expect nothing. A screen door.

Memory: the feeling of heaven or attachment to vision, mountain bright.

It's red in the fall and Friday night.

We sneak out past the county line.

Narratives left standing in for us both.

Too drunk to drive home, too calm to be engulfed in swallows.

The world think-film crackles back to present.

Excavation, Caterpillar machinery.

Dismembered parts found in the gully.

DUSK

seen before light

lining an instant
that time you
were just

a shape standing

March 18th, dark outside. You walk to my house because you don't want to move downstate.
You open my window holding a flashlight and I pray you are Christ carrying me back
somewhere I miss.

When you moved, I took it upon myself to trespass. I walked your family land and traced my fingers over the laurels. I looked for your blood in the freezing springs. I wrote in the snow, *sorry about your dad going to war* and *we will start a band someday*. I huddled with the words and imagined they were written in red in a leather-bound book which bore significance. Over the guardrail, I was carried in the smell of buck deer guts rising like Elijah called to heaven. Yesterday we were just talking, being friends, saying how funny it is this place is much older than our lives. Ice catches my face and turns every picture roughly a million years old.

CONFUSED WITH THE SAME LEAVES

the c-shaped cypress sits empty and caving in

outside windows are hazed in cornstalks

my hands become firing pistols unto the god green mountains

I hear a white and black horse galloping through my toothless face

as an infant the flowers beamed more scarce

a gap in the alphabet

human eyes rested on undeserving leaves

evening is bright orange by yonder single-wide

my grandmother slept in the creek when she returned to the mountains

twinning leaves composed of flowers rotted in the thicket

a moving of history to present

we laid around all winter together

how murky shadows become ribcages braided with root systems

do you have any memory of what makes you

hum some worried fiddle tune

on the front porch where you lost it

I'm pulling a razor blade whisker-close to the wrecked and dented ambulance boxes and trucks, stripping off glue and decals, busting out dents, and sanding away corrosion before hanging them in the paint booth of my dad's shop.

He has made his living this way since I started high school. Each day is a similar process for him and his crew of workers.

We take breaks and eat cookies and drink soda. We sit around the front desk and tell stories.

The evening folds in on itself while we are at home.

In the
woods
the hills
just wither
tectonically.

N⊙TES

Blindspot (the Rest was published as a chapbook in 2018 by Garden-Door Press. I'd like to thank Marty and Kina for their attention, support, and love.

Dusk Melody was published as a chapbook in 2019 by Shirt-Pocket Press. Thanks to Michael Sikkema for publishing and supporting my work.

I'd also like to thank the editors of the following journals for including a number of these poems and parts of these poems in their publications: *Denver Quarterly, Yalobusha Review, Word For / Word, Inter|rupture, After the Pause, Otoliths,* and *'Pider Mag.*

Excerpts from this book have previously been published in *DIAGRAM* in the form of essays after Abe Smith's *The Destruction of Man* and Nathan Hauke's *Indian Summer Recycling.* Thank you each for your inspiration, guidance, and support.

"*This book, being about work is, by its very nature, about violence—to the spirit as well as to the body*" is a quote taken from Studs Terkel's "Introduction" to *Working.*

"*There are so many revolutions light years away*" is line sixty-seven from *The Battlefield Where the Moon Says I Love You.*

"*disorder is another order*" riffs on a line by Susan Howe.

"*speech is a mouth*" is a line taken from Robert Creeley's poem, "The Language."

"*and then I laid myself to rest…*" borrows a form used by Matthew Vollmer in *Inscriptions for Headstones* (Outpost19, 2012).

Thanks to the following people for their undying love, support, grace, and patience as they were vital to the creation of this book: Jane Virginia Rohrer, Michael Martin Shea, Ashleigh Bryant Phillips, Alex Porco, Michael White, Mark Cox, Landon Gray, Howard Parsons, Kevin Chesser, Lewis Dahm, Corey Parlamento, UNCW Workshop.

This book was written while working with my father at Gray's Emergency Paint in West Jefferson, North Carolina during the summer of 2018.

BIOGRAPHY

Evan Gray lives in the Appalachian Mountains of North Carolina. He has earned a Masters of Fine Arts from the University of North Carolina at Wilmington. He currently is a Visiting Assistant Professor of English at Appalachian State University. *Thickets Swamped in Fence-Coated Briars* is his first book.

www.ingramcontent.com/pod-product-compliance
Lightning Source LLC
Chambersburg PA
CBHW040909130726
48005CB00019BA/3032